2015

They Lived with the Dinosaurs

by Russell Freedman

Holiday House · New York

To Frank Dempsey and Grafton Keane,
survivors from the prehistoric past.

Library of Congress Cataloging in Publication Data

Freedman, Russell.
They lived with the dinosaurs.

Includes index.
SUMMARY: Describes the animals now living that
are virtually unchanged from their ancestors alive
during the Age of Reptiles.
1. Living fossils—Juvenile literature.
2. Paleontology—Juvenile literature. [1. Living
fossils. 2. Fossils. 3. Animals] I. Title.
QL88.5.F68   560   80-15851
ISBN 0-8234-0424-2

These footprints were left behind by a giant dinosaur. They were found buried under a stream bed in Texas.

You can see dinosaur footprints at some museums. You can look at gigantic dinosaur skeletons. But you can never see a dinosaur in the flesh. Dinosaurs are extinct. They died out long ago.

This book is about some creatures that lived with the dinosaurs. They did not die out. They have survived since prehistoric times with little change, and they live with us today.

Dinosaur footprints from Glen Rose, Texas

When an animal dies, its body usually disappears. The flesh rots away or is eaten. Sun, rain, and frost wear down the bones. Even the bones of a mighty elephant will finally turn to dust.

Once in a great while, a dead animal is buried in mud before its bones decay. As time passes, the mud may turn to stone. When that happens, the animal's bones also turn to stone. They lie hidden in the earth as a record of the past.

These bones are called *fossils*. Footprints that have turned to stone are also fossils. A fossil is any trace of an animal or plant that lived long ago.

Scientists learn about prehistoric animals by digging up fossils. A few scattered bones or teeth can tell what an animal looked like and how it lived. Sometimes scientists are lucky enough to find an entire skeleton.

Skeleton of Diplodocus (di-PLOD-o-kus),
a giant dinosaur that lived 150 million years ago.
Diplodocus was 80 feet long and weighed 12 tons.

TIME CHART

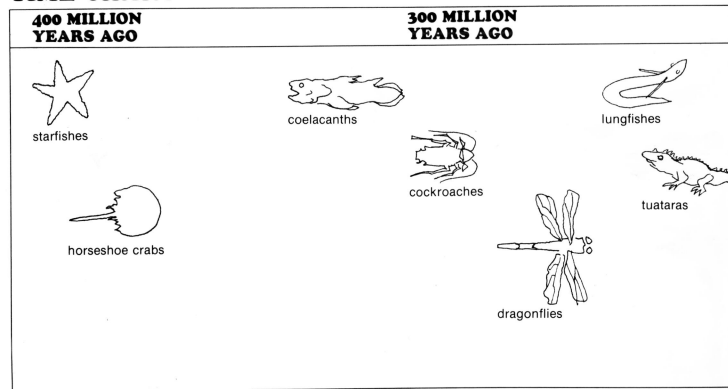

400 MILLION YEARS AGO

300 MILLION YEARS AGO

starfishes

horseshoe crabs

coelacanths

cockroaches

dragonflies

lungfishes

tuataras

The chart shows when animals described in this book lived on earth much as we see them today.

Many different kinds of animals lived with the dinosaurs. Some of them died out. They became extinct, just as the dinosaurs did.

Other animals lived on, but they changed greatly as time passed. They changed so much over millions of years, they no longer look like their ancient ancestors.

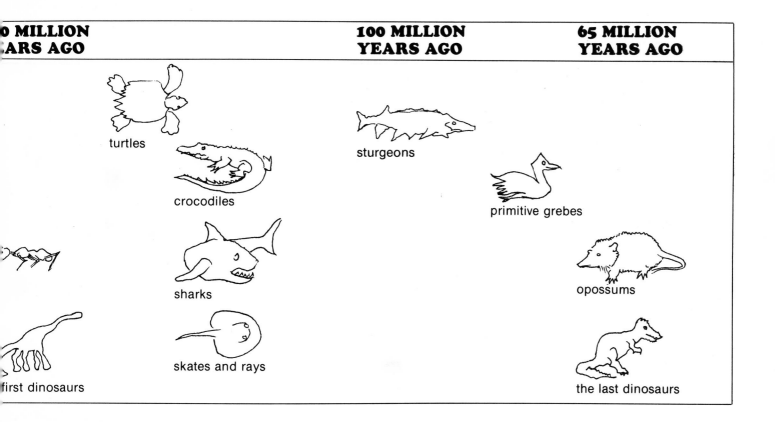

turtles

crocodiles

sturgeons

primitive grebes

sharks

opossums

skates and rays

first dinosaurs

the last dinosaurs

A few animals did not change. And they did not die out. Their way of life was so successful, they stayed much the same from one generation to the next. Today they still look and act as they did in the distant past. Some of these animals have changed so little, they are called "living fossils."

A horseshoe crab crawls across a beach at low tide.
Barnacles cling to the top of its shell.

WILLIAM M. STEPHENS

Have you ever found a horseshoe crab on the beach? If you should spot one, look at it carefully. It is one of the oldest creatures living on earth today.

Horseshoe crabs were crawling up on ancient beaches 400 million years ago. They looked the same then as they do now. They still swim through shallow water near shore, hunting for worms, clams, and dead fish. They will eat almost anything that they can shovel into their small mouths.

Their name comes from the horseshoe shape of their tough shells. As a horseshoe crab grows, it gets too big for its shell. Finally the shell splits open. The crab crawls out. It walks away with a new shell on its back, leaving the old one behind.

This ancient horseshoe crab became a fossil when it sank into mud and turned to stone. It differs from horseshoe crabs today only in size. Modern horseshoe crabs are bigger than ancient ones.

Many other familiar creatures swarmed through prehistoric seas. Giant squids darted swiftly backward—chasing their prey, grabbing them with sucker-bearing arms, and biting them to death. Brightly colored starfish crept slowly along the sea bottom, feeding on shellfish. Clams and oysters buried themselves in mud. Barnacles clung to rocks—or to the shells of horseshoe crabs.

Then as now, animals like these were common along the beaches and on the sea floor. They looked very much as they do today. And they left beautiful fossils that reveal their shapes and sizes millions of years ago.

Starfish fossil, nearly 400 million years old

SMITHSONIAN INSTITUTION

Modern starfishes

NEW YORK ZOOLOGICAL SOCIETY

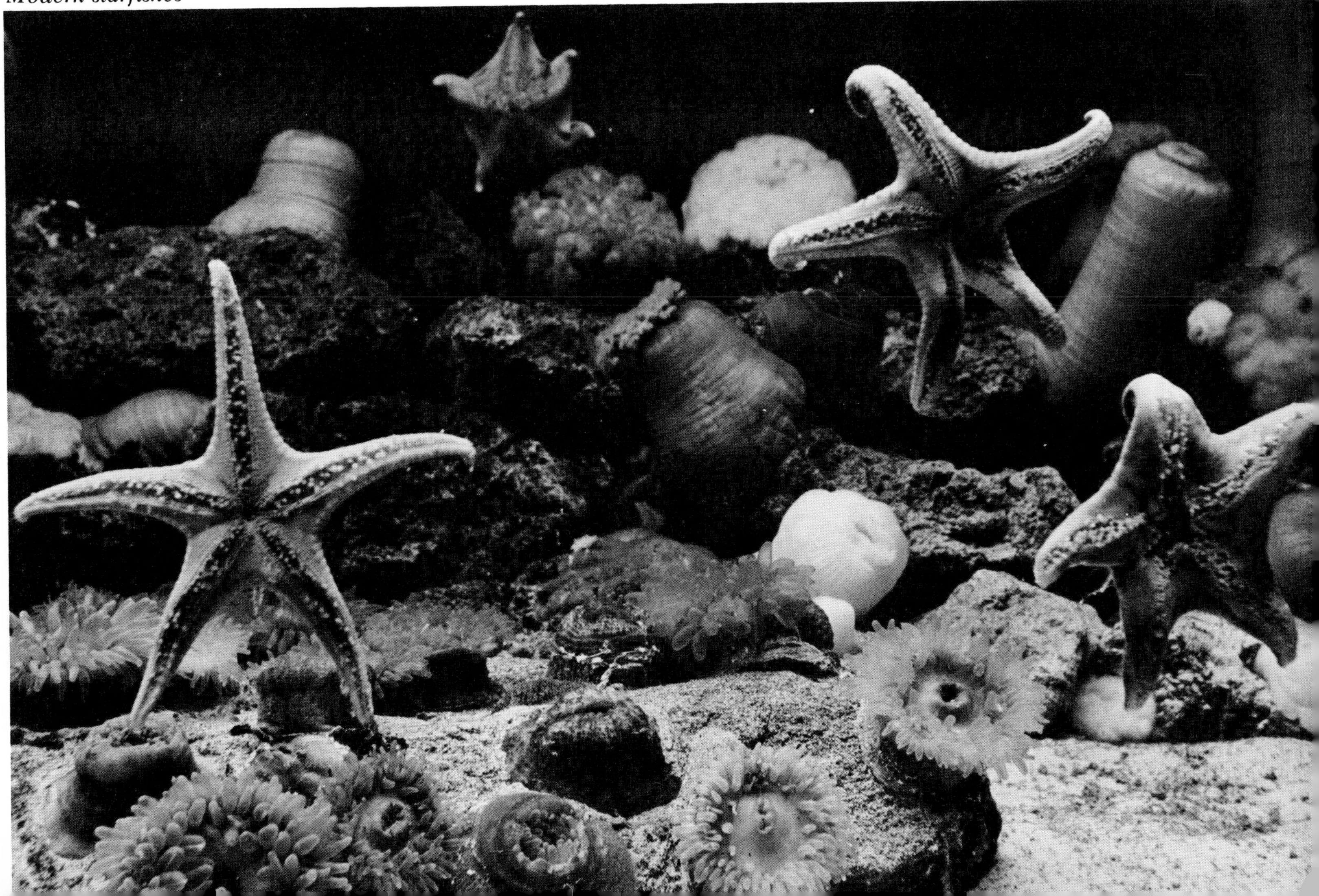

Coelacanth fossil, about 350 million years old   SMITHSONIAN INSTITUTION

Fish are the oldest animals with backbones. The earliest fishes appeared in the seas about 400 million years ago. By the time the dinosaurs came along, the seas were crowded with fishes of many kinds.

One ancient fish is called the coelacanth (SEE-la-kanth). When dinosaurs roamed the land, coelacanths were common in the seas. Then they seemed to die out. Scientists found their bones, but no one had ever seen a living coelacanth.

In 1938, fishermen in the Indian Ocean caught a strange fish about five feet long. It had bright blue scales and long, fleshy fins. Scientists who studied this fish were amazed. It was a true coelacanth—a living fossil. Coelacanths weren't extinct after all. They were survivors from the distant past.

Since then, a few other coelacanths have been caught in the Indian Ocean. They are the world's oldest living fish. For more than 300 million years, they have stayed much the same.

We know that coelacanths give birth to living young. But we don't know much about their way of life. Scientists hope to raise these fish and learn more about their ancient habits.

Modern coelacanth PEABODY MUSEUM OF NATURAL HISTORY, YALE UNIVERSITY

African lungfish gulping air

Some early fishes lived in swamps, ponds, and streams. During long periods without rain, their homes began to dry up. Sometimes only a mud puddle remained.

Many primitive fishes died out. The lungfishes survived because they grew lungs as well as gills. When the water they lived in was stale, they rose to the surface and gulped air.

They also grew long fleshy fins, like arms. During dry periods, they paddled across the land from one mud puddle to the next.

Lungfishes live today in Australia, Africa, and South America.

Modern sturgeon

Sturgeons are famous for their caviar, which is made from the female's eggs. They come from an ancient group of fishes that left few living survivors. With their huge armored bodies, they look ancient. Sturgeons like the ones we see today go back about 100 million years.

Some sturgeons live in the ocean and swim upstream to lay their eggs. Others live all year long in freshwater lakes. The biggest sturgeons are found in Russian lakes. They weigh a ton or more and may be 25 feet long.

Great white shark, commonly called the Man-eater.
This is the most dangerous of all living sharks.
Its teeth have notched edges, like steak knives.

MARINE STUDIOS, MARINELAND, FLORIDA

Sharks look like prehistoric monsters, and that's just what they are. In the days of the dinosaurs, sharks fought deadly battles with sea monsters as frightening as themselves.

16

Primitive sharks roamed the seas 350 million years ago. Some of them were 50 feet long—the size of many yachts. Modern sharks began to appear 150 million years ago. Before the dinosaurs died out, all the modern families of sharks had come into being.

They are as dangerous now as they were then. Sharks have always been attracted by the smell of blood. They strike quickly from below, tearing at their prey with rows of sharp, pointed teeth. Some sharks will attack anything that moves.

This rare shark is a living fossil called Galeus (GAY-lee-us). It belongs to a primitive group of deep-sea sharks.

The photo was taken at a depth of 3500 feet from a research submarine.

WILLIAM M.
STEPHENS

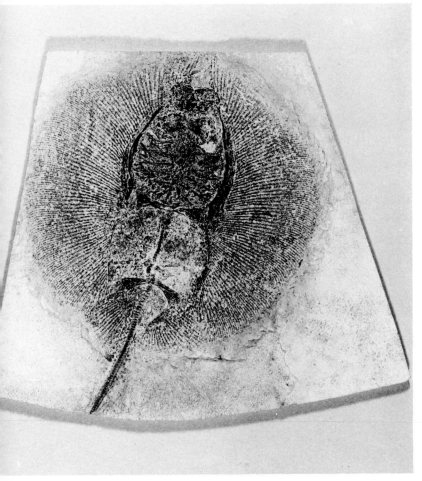

Stingray fossil. Stingrays like this one lived more than 100 million years ago. They differed little from stingrays today.

If you could visit an ancient sea, you might see a giant manta ray flapping near the water's surface. Skates and rays came into being about the same time as their relatives, the sharks. They were common in prehistoric seas, and they are common today.

You can recognize skates and rays by their flat bodies and long tails. Big fins are attached to their heads, like a pair of wings. As they flap through the water, they seem to be flying. Sometimes they bury themselves in sand.

Most skates and rays can't hurt you, but stingrays are deadly. They have sharp, poisonous spines on their tails. When they flick their tails like whips, those spines can stab and kill.

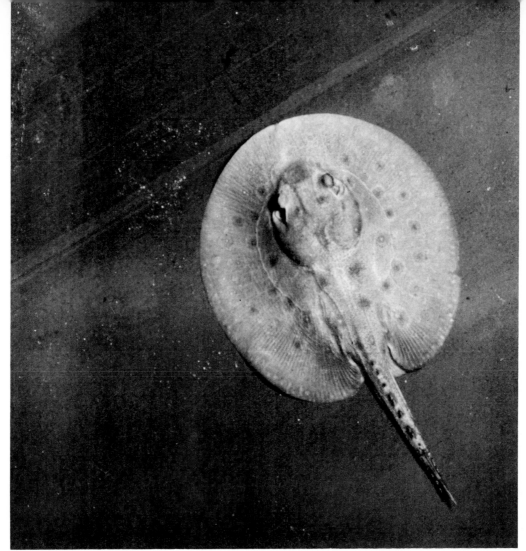

Freshwater stingray

The earliest insects crept over rocks and crawled on the ground. They had no wings. We are not sure when they appeared on earth. The first insects with wings appeared about 300 million years ago.

By the time the dinosaurs came along, insects were everywhere. Many of them would look familiar to us today. Giant dragonflies flitted over the dinosaurs' heads. Huge cockroaches zigzagged past their feet. Beetles, grasshoppers, crickets, cicadas, leafhoppers, and mayflies swarmed through the forests and jungles.

Most fossils of ancient insects show the outlines of their wings and bodies. When these insects died, they fell into ponds or streams. They sank into the mud and left faint marks, which later turned to stone.

The fossil on the opposite page shows the mark left by an ancient cricket.

Cricket fossil

Dragonfly fossil, about 250 million years old

The first flying insects could not fold their wings against their bodies. Their wings were held straight out at all times. They could fly, but they could not hide from enemies by crawling under leaves or into holes.

Most of those insects died out. Only a few insects that can't fold their wings still survive. Among them are the dragonflies.

Early dragonflies looked like the ones we see today, except for size. Some were giants with outstretched wings longer than a man's arm. Their wings measured two-and-a-half feet across.

Though dragonflies still can't fold their wings, they have survived for almost 300 million years. One reason is that they are expert fliers. They can reach 36 miles an hour in short bursts, making them the fastest insect. They change course quickly, darting and swooping. And they stop in midair, like a helicopter getting ready to land. Dragonflies chase, catch, and eat their food in the air.

Modern dragonfly

Cockroach fossil

Modern American cockroach

A modern cockroach is a small version of an ancient cockroach. It looks just like the huge roaches that prowled through hot and humid swamps 300 million years ago. Some ancient roaches were as long as your hand.

Cockroaches were among the first insects that could fold their wings. Their sleek, flat bodies make it easy for them to hide. Their long legs make them fast runners. They can eat almost anything. That is why they have survived so long with so little change.

The ant you see here was crawling up a tree trunk about 50 million years ago. It was trapped by the sticky sap that oozed out of an ancient pine tree. The sap turned into hard amber. And the ant was preserved, hairs and all.

Ants were latecomers on the insect scene, along with their relatives the bees and wasps. The earliest ants came into being nearly 200 million years ago, about the same time as the first dinosaurs. The ant shown above differs little from ants today. It has wings because it was on its mating flight.

Ancient winged ant preserved in amber

Dinosaurs appeared on earth during the Age of Reptiles. At first they were not the giants we usually think of. Most of the early dinosaurs were small. Some were no bigger than chickens.

Giant dinosaurs came along later. The terrible meat eater Tyrannosaurus (Tee-RAN-o-SAWR-us) walked on its hind legs and stood two stories tall. It was almost 50 feet long. The huge plant eater Brachiosaurus (BRAK-ee-o-SAWR-us) may have weighed 100 tons—as much as 16 full-grown elephants.

Skeleton of a flying reptile, or pterosaur. Its wings measured seven feet across.

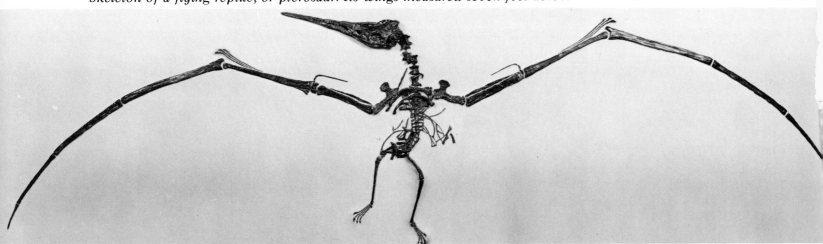

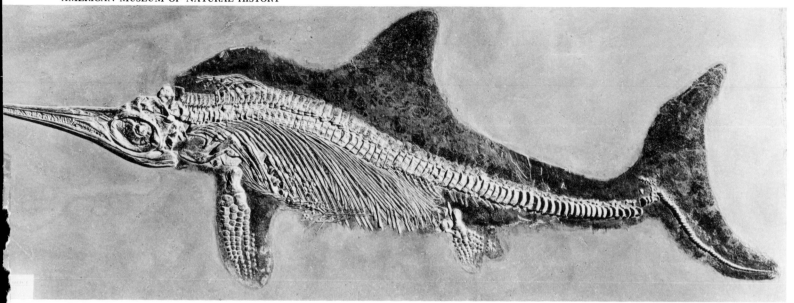

Skeleton of a sea-going reptile, or ichthyosaur. This rare fossil
shows the outline of the body as well as the skeleton.

Other strange reptiles lived at sea and in the air. Big flying reptiles called pterosaurs (TAIR-o-sawrs) flapped their leathery wings overhead. Enormous sea-going reptiles called ichthyosaurs (IK-thee-o-sawrs) and plesiosaurs (PLEEZ-ee-o-sawrs) paddled through the oceans.

Most of the reptiles that lived then have long since disappeared. They exist today as skeletons in museums. But a few reptiles from that long-ago age did not die out with the others. They have survived to the present day.

Most people have never seen the rare creature shown here. It is called a tuatara (too-uh-TAR-uh). The name means "bearing spines." It comes from the spiny crest on the tuatara's back.

The tuatara is not a lizard, though it looks like one. It belongs to an ancient group of reptiles that once were common. Now all the members of that group are gone—except for the tuatara. Alone among its relatives, it has survived almost unchanged for over 200 million years.

During the Age of Reptiles, tuataras lived in many parts of the world. Today they are found only on a few small islands off the coast of New Zealand, where they have no natural enemies. Their homes are underground burrows. At night they come out to feed on insects and worms. The males are about two feet long, the females shorter. It is believed that tuataras may live to be 100 years old or more.

Only a few thousand tuataras are left in the world. Their direct ancestors saw the first dinosaurs that lived on earth, and they saw the last dinosaurs die out.

A tuatara at the entrance to its underground burrow

Turtles have been protected by their hard shells for 175 million years. They haven't changed much since then.

They can live almost anywhere—in deserts or swamps, in small ponds or open oceans. They can stay underwater for hours without breathing air. They can eat almost anything from lizards to leaves. And they can go a year or more without eating.

Archelon (AR-kee-lawn), the biggest turtle of all time, swam through the seas about 100 million years ago. It was 11 feet long and 12 feet across at the flippers. Its shell was part bone and part tough, leathery skin.

The skeleton of Archelon shown here has a hind flipper missing. It was probably bitten off by an ancient sea monster.

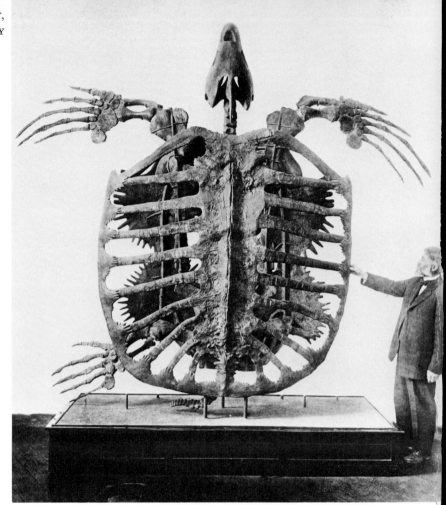

Skeleton of the giant turtle Archelon

Modern loggerhead turtle. Loggerheads belong to a group of turtles that go back more than 100 million years.

This early crocodile, Mystriosaurus (MIS-tree-o-SAWR-us), lived about 150 million years ago.

Of all the animals living today, the closest relatives of the dinosaurs are members of the crocodile family.

Crocodiles and dinosaurs had the same ancestors. They came from a group of early reptiles that walked upright on their hind legs.

Many dinosaurs also walked upright. They used their long tails as a balance.

Crocodiles, like dinosaurs, have hind legs that are longer than their front ones. When moving slowly, a crocodile crawls with its belly on the ground. But it can also walk and even run with surprising speed. And when it raises itself high on its legs, it actually looks like a dinosaur.

For the past 150 million years, crocodiles have lived in and near the water. They drift along with only their eyes and nostrils showing, disguised as floating logs. When some unlucky creature comes too close, they grab it with their powerful jaws.

Nile crocodile

The earliest known bird fluttered from tree to tree about 140 million years ago. Actually, it was part reptile and part bird. It had a lizard's head, a long tail, and clawed fingers at the tips of its wings. But it also had feathers.

It probably did not fly very well. Perhaps it ran along the ground and climbed up rocks and trees with its clawed wings. Then it took off and glided for short distances. It is called Archaeopteryx (ar-kee-OP-ter-iks), which means "ancient wing."

Later, other birds appeared that were less like reptiles and more like true birds. By the end of the dinosaur era, birds were common.

Fossil of Archaeopteryx, the earliest known bird, showing an imprint of its skeleton and feathers. Archaeopteryx was about the size of a crow.

Scientists have found fossils of primitive loons, grebes, herons, pelicans, flamingos, sandpipers, and other birds that lived 60 or 70 million years ago. None of these birds looked exactly like their modern relatives. But they resembled them. And they were flying overhead when the last dinosaurs rumbled across the land.

This Chilean grebe belongs to a primitive group of birds that has changed little in 80 million years.

NEW YORK ZOOLOGICAL SOCIETY

Every so often, small furry creatures raced past the feet of the dinosaurs. They were the earliest mammals—warm-blooded animals that nurse their young.

Mammals had been living on earth almost as long as the dinosaurs. At first they were no bigger than rats and mice. They seemed lost among the giant reptiles that still ruled the earth.

Gradually the mammals spread. Some stayed in the dense undergrowth of tropical jungles. Others took to the safety of the trees. They fed on insects, grubs, fruits, and eggs. When they had a chance, they stole dinosaur eggs. And they moved about quickly, watching out for their enemies.

Fossil of an ancient opossum

Modern North American opossum

Before the dinosaurs died out, many different kinds of mammals had appeared. They fell into two main groups. Some were swift insect eaters like shrews. They hid their babies in nests while they were nursing them. Others were pouched animals like opossums. They carried their babies in a pouch on the mother's belly.

Most of the mammals that lived then have changed greatly. But opossums have survived almost unchanged. Modern opossums look very much like their ancestors from the days of the dinosaurs.

37

About 65 million years ago, the dinosaurs vanished. We do not know why. They disappeared along with many other kinds of animals. We call this period "the time of the great dying."

The giant reptiles were gone, but some reptiles survived. Crocodiles still basked in the sun. Turtles paddled through the seas and buried themselves in mud. By now there were modern lizards scurrying about and big snakes like pythons.

Other groups of animals also lived on. Modern fishes like salmon and herring swam through the oceans. Familiar insects filled the fields and woods. And the first modern groups of birds were just beginning to appear.

The mammals—those small furry creatures—were spreading fast. They were about to take the places of the great reptiles that had ruled the earth for so long. During the next 65 million years, they would give rise to dogs and cats, horses and elephants, monkeys and apes, and all the other mammals we know today.

The Age of Reptiles had ended. The Age of Mammals was about to begin. That is the age we live in now.

Footprints of the giant dinosaur Brontosaurus (BRON-toe-SAWR-us)

Index